Contents

- 2 Nouns
- 3 Plurals
- 4 Vowel endings
- 5 Verbs
- 6 Nouns and verbs
- 7 Commas in complex sentences
- 8 Word roots
- 9 Spelling rules
- 10 Prefixes
- 11 Synonyms
- 12 Idioms
- 13 Dialogue
- 14 Adverbs and dialogue
- 15 Writing plays
- 16 Homophones
- 17 Suffixes
- 18 Antonyms
- 19 Onomatopoeia
- 20 Metaphorical expressions
- 21 Personal pronouns
- 22 Subordinate clauses
- 23 The narrator
- 24 Words from other languages
- 25 Word origins
- 26 Prepositions
- 27 Possessive apostrophes
- 28 Making notes
- 29 Possessive pronouns
- 30 Punctuation
- 31 Unstressed vowels
- 32 Answers

AGES 9–10
KEY STAGE 2

Premier ENGLISH

Nouns

A **noun** names a thing or a feeling.

Common nouns name a person or thing.

Abstract nouns name a feeling or idea.

sheep   man   love   anger

I Sort the words in the box into common nouns and abstract nouns.

Common nouns	Abstract nouns
_____	_____
_____	_____
_____	_____
_____	_____
_____	_____

hatred   coat
fear   darkness
night   lion
jealousy   school
height
knowledge
house   bus
expertise   joy

II Look at each abstract noun. Then write a sentence that includes it.

a sympathy   _____

b hope   _____

c gratitude _____

d strength   _____

e despair   _____

f depth   _____

g courage   _____

h comfort   _____

Plurals

Plural means **two or more** of something.

Most plurals end in s.

Words ending s, x, sh, or ch usually end es.

Words ending with a consonant followed by y end ies.

cats

foxes

babies

I Underline the correctly spelt word in each group.

a patchs   patchies   patches

b toys   toyes   toyies

c worrys   worries   worryes

d trys   tryes   tries

e penes   pennes   pens

f dishes   dishs   dishies

g citys   cityes   cities

h caks   cakes   cakies

II Write down the plurals of these words.

a hat   _____

b party   _____

c bush   _____

d box   _____

e lorry   _____

f bus   _____

g tree   _____

h cry   _____

i book   _____

j puppy   _____

Vowel endings

Most words that end with a vowel end in e, but some words end in a, i, o or u.

banana

spaghetti

domino

emu

Most of these words end in s in the plural and some, like spaghetti, are the same in the singular and in the plural. But some words that end in o end in es in the plural, like *buffaloes* and *dominoes*.

I Choose a, i, o or u to complete these words.

a past____   h viol____

b cobr____   i risott____

c pian____   j em____

d chapatt____ k pizz____

e gn____   l zebr____

f cell____   m camer____

g tub____   n are____

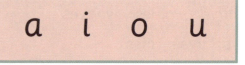

II Write the plural of these words. You will need to decide whether each one should end in s or es.

a zoo _____   f hero _____

b radio _____   g domino _____

c echo _____   h disco _____

d solo _____   i yo yo _____

e kimono _____ j cuckoo _____

Verbs

Verbs describe actions. Some verbs are active and some are passive.

Robbie **blew** out the candle.

Robbie **was blown** over by the wind.

This verb is **active**. It describes what Robbie does.

This verb is **passive**. It explains what happens to Robbie.

I Underline the verb in each sentence. Then tick the box to say whether you think it is active or passive.

		active verb	passive verb
a	Katie fell over.	☐	☐
b	Ben ate the chips.	☐	☐
c	The window was broken when the ball hit it.	☐	☐
d	Mia picked a flower.	☐	☐
e	The winning story was written by Jake.	☐	☐
f	Mum drove me to school.	☐	☐
g	Our house was built three years ago.	☐	☐
h	The letter was delivered by the postman.	☐	☐
i	We ran home quickly.	☐	☐
j	The door was slammed by John.	☐	☐

II Write sentences using these verbs.

a played _____

b was played _____

c found _____

d be found _____

e saw _____

f were seen _____

g bought _____

h was bought _____

Nouns and verbs

All sentences contain a noun or pronoun and a verb.

If the noun is **singular**, you must use the singular verb form.

If the noun is **plural**, you must use the plural form of the verb.

singular noun   singular verb form
The cat plays with the ball.

plural noun   plural verb form
The cats play with the ball.

I Choose the correct verb form from the words in bold to match each noun.

a The girls _____ netball. **plays   play**

b The rabbits _____ the grass. **nibble   nibbles**

c She _____ every day. **swims   swim**

d The children _____ the sweets. **gobbles   gobble**

e The birds _____ away. **fly   flies**

f Apples _____ on trees. **grows   grow**

g We _____ late. **are   am**

h My bike _____ mending. **needs   need**

II Choose a verb from the box to complete each sentence. Make sure you use the correct form of the verb you choose.

a The dog _____ its tail.

b Postmen _____ letters.

c A cow _____ grass.

d In winter it _____ very cold.

e Pandas _____ bamboo.

f Santa Claus _____ presents.

g Cats _____ mice.

h Weekends _____ great!

chase
delivers
eat
are
eats
deliver
chases
is

Commas in complex sentences

Complex sentences contain more than one clause. Commas help to separate these clauses.

The main clause gives us the key information.

The subordinate clause gives us extra information.

I **Underline the main clause in each sentence.**

a It was hot, so we had a cold drink.

b My birthday is in October, just before Hallowe'en.

c On Friday, we are going on holiday.

d Because it was so dark, we took a torch.

e We flew to Greece, on an aeroplane.

f Susie is my best friend, although I haven't known her very long.

g The window got broken, but it was an accident.

h The shop was shut, so we couldn't buy any sweets.

II **Add commas to each sentence to separate the main and subordinate clauses. Then underline the main clause.**

a It was raining hard so I took an umbrella.

b The bus was late so we had to walk.

c Because it was Saturday we could play football all day.

d Max has chickenpox so he has to stay at home.

e I play the guitar although I'm not very good.

f Mum lost her keys so we had to call a locksmith.

g Dad drank all the tea so he had to buy some more.

h The television broke down so I read my book.

Word roots

Lots of the words we use come from other words.

approve → approval

approve → disapprove

This can help us with spelling.

I Write down two words from the box against each word root.

> boring   relative   building   machinist   impress   lightning   breakfast
> operation   depression   rebuild   delight   breakable   cooperate
> machinery   relation   boredom

a bore _____ _____   e break _____ _____

b light _____ _____   f operate _____ _____

c press _____ _____   g relate _____ _____

d machine _____ _____   h build _____ _____

II Write down two words that come from each of these root words.

a act _____ _____

b take _____ _____

c electric _____ _____

d sign _____ _____

e claim _____ _____

f public _____ _____

g cover _____ _____

h child _____ _____

Spelling rules

Following spelling rules can help us to spell whole families of words. One useful rule helps us to add full to words. Another helps us to spell words containing a soft c sound.

When you use full as a suffix, the final ll becomes l.

When the letter c makes a soft sound, it is usually followed by i.

play**ful** beauti**ful** **c**innamon a**c**cident

 Underline examples of the spelling rules above in these sentences.

a It was peaceful in the woods.

b I can't decide which book to read.

c I love living in a city.

d Gemma was careful when she crossed the road.

e The runners ran three circuits of the track.

f Kelvin was fearful he would be discovered.

g We are learning about decimals in maths.

h I am hopeful that I'll win the competition.

 Now use the spelling rules to find the incorrect spelling in each sentence. Underline the incorrect word, then write it correctly in the space.

a We saw a great film at the sinema. _____

b I love colourfull clothes. _____

c Some berries are harmfull if you eat them. _____

d There were clowns at the sircus. _____

e It is rude to speak with a mouthfull of cake. _____

f I made a difficult desision. _____

g The ballerina was very gracefull. _____

h We sat in a sircle. _____

Prefixes

We can add prefixes to the **beginning** of words to change their meaning. Different prefixes have different meanings.

bi + plane = biplane

bi means two, so a biplane is a plane with two sets of wings.

I Complete these word sums.

a auto + graph = _____

b circum + ference = _____

c bi + focals = _____

d tele + photo = _____

e trans + parent = _____

f bi + lingual = _____

g circum + stance = _____

h trans + plant = _____

i auto + biography = _____

j tele + graph = _____

II Choose a prefix from the box to complete each word sum.

a <u>tele</u>   + phone = <u>telephone</u>

b _____ + cycle = _____

c _____ + matic = _____

d _____ + late = _____

e _____ + lingual = _____

f _____ + mobile = _____

g _____ + vision = _____

h _____ + fer = _____

auto
bi
tele
trans

Synonyms

Synonyms are words that have similar meanings.

happy   joyful   excited   contented

Using synonyms can make your writing more interesting, but be careful to choose ones with exactly the right meaning.

I Choose the best synonym from the words in bold to complete each sentence.

a It was a _____ summer's day. **hot   steaming**

b When my cup was _____ I asked for more juice. **hollow   empty**

c Mr Fisher was _____ when I forgot my homework. **angry   frustrated**

d The hedgehog is a _____ animal. **ferocious   wild**

e Ranjit was _____ at the dentist. **brave   heroic**

f I threw away my _____ toys. **ancient   old**

g At the end of the race I was _____. **exhausted   sleepy**

h I _____ the vase by mistake. **broke   destroyed**

II Write a sentence using each of these synonyms.

a chilly   _____

b freezing _____

c cold   _____

d icy   _____

e cool   _____

f frosty   _____

Idioms

We sometimes say things like:

'Jo opened a can of worms.'   or   'Alex and Kim are like two peas in a pod.'

We don't literally mean what we say. These phrases are called idioms.

I   Draw lines to match up these common sayings (idioms) with their meanings.

a out of order   happens very rarely

b under the weather   just like a parent

c peas in a pod   absolutely thrilled

d over the moon   feeling unwell

e worth her salt   a great person to have around

f a chip off the old block raining very hard

g it's raining cats and dogs very similar

h once in a blue moon   not acceptable

II   Write a sentence using each of these idioms.

a right as rain

_____

b sleeping like a log

_____

c never in a month of Sundays

_____

d paint the town red

_____

e keep your eyes peeled

_____

f down in the dumps

_____

Dialogue

When characters in a story **talk to each other**, we call it dialogue. When you write dialogue you need to follow rules, so your readers know who is saying what.

We put what our characters say in speech marks. We also start a new line when a different person speaks.

'I've lost my bike,' complained Martin.

'Where did you leave it?' asked Mrs Chaudri.

I **Add the speech marks to this piece of dialogue.**

a Do you want to come back to my house after school? asked Jamie.

b That would be great, replied Sasha. I'll have to check with my mum though.

c OK. If she says yes we could play with my new computer game.

d I'll go and ask her now, said Sasha. See you in a minute.

II **Write this conversation as dialogue, including speech marks.**

Dad: Have you done your homework?

John: Not all of it.

Dad: You'll have to do the rest after tea.

John: But I'm supposed to be playing football with Stephen.

Dad: Well, Stephen will just have to wait while you finish your homework.

_____
_____
_____
_____
_____
_____
_____
_____

Adverbs and dialogue

Dialogue is the name given to a conversation between characters in a story.

Kelly said, 'It's my birthday soon.'
'Are you having a party?' replied Ashley.

Adverbs tell us **how** the characters talk, which can tell us a lot about how they are feeling.

'Yes, it's going to be great!' said Kelly, **excitedly**.

I Choose an adverb from the box to complete each sentence.

a 'I won first prize!' said Mary _____.
b 'Excuse me,' whispered Phil _____.
c 'I want more!' demanded Owen _____.
d 'I'm sure I'll win,' said Ruby _____.
e 'I bet it will rain tomorrow,' complained Sam _____.
f 'You're late,' barked Mr Moor _____.
g 'I'm tired,' yawned Connor _____.
h 'It's not fair!' complained Ella _____.

gloomily
crossly
timidly
sleepily
confidently
rudely
proudly
sulkily

II Write sensible dialogue to complete this conversation. Look at the adverbs to give you clues about what Dad and Ben might be saying.

a '_____?' asked Dad patiently.
b '_____,' replied Ben stubbornly.
c '_____,' repeated Dad firmly.
d '_____,' muttered Ben quietly.
e '_____?' asked Dad angrily.
f '_____,' replied Ben tearfully.
g '_____,' said Dad wearily.
h '_____,' sniffed Ben sulkily.

Writing plays

Plays tell stories, just like a book. A play script gives the actors performing the play the information they need to act out the story.

> [Beth's room, at night. Beth asleep in bed. A crash is heard off-stage]
>
> Beth [sitting up]: What was that?
>
> [Beth creeps to the door and listens. She is wearing pyjamas.] Sarah, are you awake?
>
> Sarah [sleepily]: No, I'm not!

The settings and costumes are described.

Stage directions tell the actors what to do and how to behave.

The dialogue tells them what to say.

 Imagine you are writing a play script based on the following section of text. Write a description of the setting, and stage directions for Beth and Sarah.

> Beth crept to her sister's room. 'Sarah, wake up!' she whispered. Sarah rolled over and awoke slowly.
>
> 'What is it?' she grumbled.
>
> 'I can hear someone downstairs,' hissed Beth, creeping back to the door to listen.

Setting: _____

_____

Stage directions for Beth: _____

Stage directions for Sarah: _____

II Decide what you think happens next in the story. Then write the next few lines of the play, including dialogue and stage directions.

_____

_____

_____

_____

_____

_____

_____

Homophones

Homophones are words that sound the same, but are spelt differently and have different meanings.

knight

night

We need to be sure we pick the correct homophone to fit the sentence we are writing.

The **knight** rode bravely into battle.

As **night** fell, the moon came up.

I Write down homophones for these words.

a cereal _____   d waist _____

b allowed _____   e hymn _____

c bored _____   f beach _____

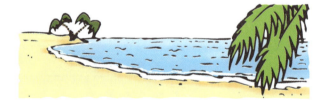

g steal _____

h tail _____

i leak _____

j week _____

II Read this paragraph then circle the correct homophone from each pair in bold.

We took our **fair fare** and went to **bye buy** a ticket for the boat trip. The **son sun** shone brightly as our boat docked at the **quay key**. A sailor with blonde **hair hare** **through threw** a long **peace piece** of rope to another sailor standing by us. He **tide tied** it in a huge **not knot** to secure the boat. When the **mane main** gangplank appeared, the passengers began to **board bored** the boat. We couldn't **weight wait** to set off!

Suffixes

We can add a suffix to the end of some words to change their meaning.

Lots of words end with suffixes that make a shun sound. Several suffixes make this sound.

physi**cian**
cian

explo**sion**
sion

se**ssion**
ssion

reduc**tion**
tion

I Choose cian, sion, ssion or tion to complete these word sums. Watch out for your spelling!

a politic + _____cian_____ = _____

b confuse + _____ = _____

c direct + _____ = _____

d discuss + _____ = _____

e educate + _____ = _____

f possess + _____ = _____

g optic + _____ = _____

h transfuse + _____ = _____

II Look carefully at the words in the box. Use them to help you decide which rule refers to each of the shun suffixes in the box. Then write down the correct suffix (ssion, sion, cian, tion) next to each rule.

Rules	Suffix
a Used where words end in c. Common in occupations.	_____
b Used where the base word ends in d or de; or s or se.	_____
c Makes a clear, soft sh sound.	_____
d Used where the other rules don't apply, making it the most common shun ending.	_____

magician
electrician
extension
explosion
passion
mission
fraction
reduction
fiction

17

Antonyms

Antonyms are words that have opposite meanings.

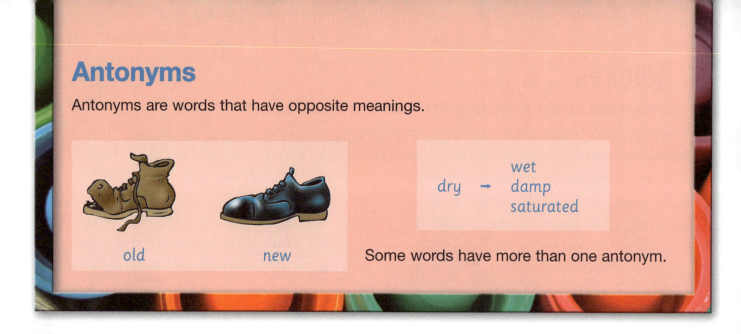

old   new

dry → wet / damp / saturated

Some words have more than one antonym.

I Draw lines to join up the pairs of antonyms.

a	late		clean
b	old		wide
c	bright		short
d	dirty		disapprove
e	grateful		dull
f	narrow		slow
g	happy		early
h	long		ungrateful
i	fast		new
j	approve		unhappy

II Think of antonyms to fill the gaps in the story. Try not to use the same antonym twice.

Goldilocks found the bears' cottage in the woods and went inside. She tried the porridge. The **big** bear's porridge was too **hot**. The _____ bear's porridge was too _____. She sat down. The **big** bear's chair was too **high**. The _____ bear's chair was too _____. She tried their beds. The **big** bear's bed was too **hard**. The _____ bear's bed was too _____. Goldilocks fell **asleep**, but when the bears returned she was wide _____ immediately. The bears chased Goldilocks away. She ran **fast** and they were too _____ to catch her.

Onomatopoeia

Onomatopoeia means words that sound the same as the noises they describe.

hiss

hoot

They are very powerful describing words.

I **Pick a word from the box to complete each sentence.**

a The wind _____ in the trees.

b Dry leaves _____ underfoot.

c The piglet _____ .

d The bell _____ to mark the hour.

e My chair fell over with a _____ .

f The jelly _____ as I spooned it into my bowl.

g The tap _____ .

h We _____ in the puddles.

> splashed
> dripped
> whispers
> crunch
> clanged
> squealed
> squelched
> crash

II **Write down what you think might be making these noises. Use the sound of the words to help you decide.**

a ping _____

b rip _____

c clatter _____

d shatter _____

e crunch _____

f rustle _____

g squeak _____

h fizz _____

Metaphorical expressions

A metaphor is where a writer describes something as if it were something else.

He was the black sheep of the family.

 Match up these metaphors with their meanings.

a She is a loose cannon. She is a good person.

b She is a good egg. We are treating ourselves.

c He is a closed book. She can't be trusted.

d We have a skeleton in the cupboard. She is unpredictable.

e We're pushing the boat out. He is annoying.

f She is a wolf in sheep's clothing. We have a family secret.

g He is a pain in the neck. She is trustworthy.

h She is a safe pair of hands. He is difficult to understand.

 Write down what you think each expression means.

a There's a bad apple in every barrel. _____

b He's a rock. _____

c Every cloud has a silver lining. _____

d She's a snake in the grass. _____

e He's like a bull in a china shop. _____

f You're an angel. _____

Personal pronouns

Pronouns take the place of a noun. They can save us from having to repeat the same noun again and again.

Personal pronouns replace proper nouns, like the names of people.

> Sam ate his crisps. **He** likes salt and vinegar flavour best.

They can also replace plural nouns that describe people or animals.

> **We** fed the rabbits. **They** love carrots.

I Underline the personal pronouns in these sentences.

a She has long hair.
b They were late.
c Mum brought us some drinks.
d We played football.
e Phone me later.
f I am ten years old.
g Are you going to the party?
h Tim watched them carefully.

II Write these sentences again, replacing the nouns in bold type with a personal pronoun.

a Susie is my friend and **Susie** lives next door.
_____

b The boys jumped on their bikes, because **the boys** didn't want to be late.
_____

c Sam and I bought some sweets and **Sam and I** had a bag each.
_____

d Jo and I went to the cinema and **Jo and I** bought some popcorn.
_____

e Mum and Dad left us with Gran last night, so **Mum and Dad** could go out.
_____

f Dad collects my sisters from school and then takes **my sisters** to Brownies.
_____

Subordinate clauses

A complex sentence has more than one clause. The main clause gives us the key information. The subordinate clause gives us extra information.

In some complex sentences, the subordinate clause is embedded in the sentence.

We use commas to separate the subordinate clause from the rest of the sentence.

The cat, **which was black**, ran up the tree.

subordinate clause

I Underline the embedded subordinate clause in each complex sentence.

a My friend, who is called Chris, is coming to tea.

b Tomorrow, after lunch, we are going to the zoo.

c My brother, who is older than me, is great at football.

d Yesterday, because it was hot, we went to the beach.

e Our teacher, Mrs Brooks, marked our books.

f The new cinema, in town, has five screens.

g Donuts, with holes in, are my favourite cakes.

h A letter, with American stamps, came for me today.

II Write these pairs of sentences again as one sentence, using an embedded subordinate clause.

a My uncle is coming to visit. He is from Australia.

My uncle, who is from Australia, is coming to visit.

b Tomorrow we are going bowling. We will go after school.

_____

c The train was crowded. It was late.

_____

d The dog chased its tail. It is called Patch.

_____

e The new coat is really warm. It is blue.

_____

f Next week we are going on holiday. We are going on Tuesday.

_____

The narrator

When we read a story, we are reading the narrator's viewpoint.

Sometimes the narrator is one of the characters in the story.

> I wish I could go to the ball.

Sometimes the narrator is not in the story at all.

> Cinderella wished she could go to the ball.

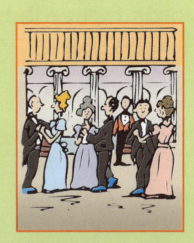

 Read this story. Then tick the box to say who you think the narrator is.

I used to be so worried. I had no money to buy food or new leather to make shoes to sell. One night I cut up the last piece of leather ready to sew the next morning and went to bed hungry. The next morning I awoke to find the finest pair of boots on the table. I sold the boots for a good price and bought more leather. That night the same thing happened again, and soon I was rich. One night I stayed awake and watched, and saw two tiny elves making the boots for me. I made them new clothes and boots to say thank you.

The narrator is not in the story. ☐

The narrator is the shoemaker. ☐

The narrator is one of the elves. ☐

II **Rewrite the story of the elves and shoemaker from the point of view of a narrator, who is not a character in the story.**

_____
_____
_____
_____
_____
_____
_____
_____
_____

Words from other languages

We use lots of words that are borrowed from other languages.

pizza

Pizza is an Italian word.

bungalow

Bungalow is an Indian word.

I Look at the words in the box. Then list all the foods. Use a dictionary to help you.

macaroni   mango   sonata   biryani   risotto   bongo   chapatti   tortilla
tombola   sauna   chalet   duvet   chow mein   gala   moussaka   cargo

_____   _____
_____   _____
_____   _____
_____   _____

II Choose which country in the box each word comes from. Then write a sentence for each word.

Italy   India   Australia
France   China

a ballet   _____
_____

b pasta   _____
_____

c koala   _____
_____

d wok   _____
_____

e tandoori _____
_____

Word origins

Lots of the words we use started out as longer words.

Some words have letters missed out.

of the clock → o'clock

Some are used without their prefixes or suffixes.

telephone → phone

Some are abbreviations or acronyms – they are made up from the initial letter of each word in a phrase.

compact disc → CD

 Match up these words with their longer forms.

a Hallowe'en — public house

b PC — salt and vinegar

c HGV — aeroplane

d pub — hire purchase

e salt 'n' vinegar — omnibus

f plane — heavy goods vehicle

g HP — personal computer

h bus — all hallows' eve

 Write down the longer forms of these words.

a TV _____

b photo _____

c PE _____

d fish 'n' chips _____

e bike _____

f VIP _____

g MP _____

h fridge _____

i UK _____

Prepositions

Prepositions describe the relationship between two people or things.

The letters dropped **onto** the mat.

I brought the book **for** you.

I **Underline the prepositions in each sentence.**

a I kicked the ball over the fence.

b Dan peered through the window.

c Lily got a postcard from Amber.

d I went to Will's house after school.

e I found the missing shoe under my bed.

f Mark threw the rubbish into the bin.

g I sat between Jenny and Ellie.

h Jack hung his coat on a peg.

II **Write down a suitable preposition to complete each sentence.**

a We hid _____ the door.

b The bird flew _____ the house.

c Mum put a photo _____ the frame.

d The frog hopped _____ the pond.

e My teacher wrote _____ the whiteboard.

f The train rushed _____ the tunnel.

g We put a star _____ the Christmas tree.

h The cat walked _____ the wall.

Possessive apostrophes

Apostrophes can be used to show that something belongs to a person or thing.

Kate's house.

The men's cars.

The boy's bags.

The babies' toys.

With singular or collective nouns, the apostrophe goes before the s.

With plural nouns, the apostrophe goes after the s.

I Add the apostrophe to the nouns in these sentences.

a A dogs tail.
b The womens shopping.
c A girls books.
d Two boys socks.
e Four horses stables.
f The peoples cheers.
g A cooks apron.
h A cats kittens.

II Write these phrases again, making all the nouns plural and placing the apostrophe in the correct place.

a The cow's field.   _The cows' fields._
b The teacher's pupil.   _____
c The child's room.   _____
d The dog's kennel.   _____
e The hen's egg.   _____
f The baker's cake.   _____
g The man's shoe.   _____
h The car's tyre.   _____

27

Making notes

When we make notes, we only need to write down the key words. These key words will remind us later about other details.

Camels are specially adapted for desert living. They have soft, wide feet to help them walk in sand. Long eyelashes keep the sand out of their eyes. Their fatty humps store water.

camels
- adapted for desert
- wide feet
- long eyelashes
- fatty humps

 Look for the key words in this paragraph. Then write your own notes.

Dinosaurs have been extinct for millions of years. We know about them from fossils found in rocks. Some dinosaurs ate meat and some ate plants. Some lived on land, some could fly and some lived in the water.

_____
_____
_____
_____
_____

 Use this set of notes to write a paragraph about castles.

Castles
- defensive
- tall, thick walls
- built on hills – good view of enemy approach
- towers in walls – arrow slits

_____
_____
_____
_____

Possessive pronouns

We use possessive pronouns in the place of nouns to tell our readers that something belongs to a person or thing.

Kate picked up **her** coat.

The boys put on **their** boots.

When we use them, we must make sure we use the right form. Kate is a girl, so we use the singular female pronoun **her**.

There are lots of boys, so we use the plural pronoun **their**.

 Draw lines to match up the two halves of each sentence.

a The cat licked   his throne.
b Ben wrote to   their song.
c Sarah drank   its field.
d The king sat on   her juice.
e The bull charged across our favourite film.
f The girls read   his pen pal.
g We watched   their books.
h They sang   its paws.

Choose a possessive pronoun to complete these sentences.
Remember, the possessive pronoun **its** does not have an apostrophe!

a Sally visited _____ friend.
b They ate _____ packed lunches.
c Kieran finished _____ homework.
d We opened _____ presents.
e The spider scuttled across _____ web.
f I tidied _____ bedroom.
g They missed _____ bus.
h The bird flew to _____ nest.

Punctuation

Punctuation marks help our readers make sense of our writing.

, Commas mark pauses in sentences, by separating clauses.

. Full stops mark the end of sentences.

! Exclamation marks can be used instead of full stops to show surprise, anger, joy or fear.

? Question marks can also be used instead of full stops, to mark the end of a question.

I Rewrite these sentences, putting the punctuation marks in the correct place.

a After all, the hunting we found the key.

b My favourite subject at school. is geography

c It was great! on holiday

d We tidied up then, got ready to go home.

e What time? is it

f Before, school we walked the dog.

II Add the punctuation and speech marks to this passage. The capital letters should give you some clues.

Last September we moved house Our new house is brilliant I remember when Mum said we were going to move Why I asked She said Our new house will have more space and a bigger garden She was right Now we have lots of space and my best friend who is called Julie lives next door

Unstressed vowels

Many words with two or more syllables contain vowels that are difficult to hear when you say the word out loud. This can make the words tricky to spell.

literature

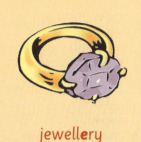

jewellery

I Underline the unstressed vowel in these words.

a general
b separate
c prosperous
d interested
e memorable
f offering

g difference
h library
i fastener
j desperate
k boundary
l conservatory

m generous
n history
o dangerous
p mystery

q boisterous
r christening
s listening
t stationery

II Correct the spelling of these words by writing them again, adding the unstressed vowel.

a frightning   _____
b busness   _____
c factry   _____
d explanatry   _____
e categry   _____
f confrence   _____
g refrence   _____
h voluntry   _____
i happning   _____
j litracy   _____

ANSWERS

Page 2
I Common nouns are: coat, darkness, night, lion, school, house, bus.
Abstract nouns are: hatred, fear, jealousy, height, knowledge, expertise, joy.

II Many answers are possible.

Page 3
I
- a patches
- b toys
- c worries
- d tries
- e pens
- f dishes
- g cities
- h cakes

II
- a hats
- b parties
- c bushes
- d boxes
- e lorries
- f buses
- g trees
- h cries
- i books
- j puppies

Page 4
I
- a pasta
- b cobra
- c piano
- d chapatti
- e gnu
- f cello
- g tuba
- h viola
- i risotto
- j emu
- k pizza
- l zebra
- m camera
- n area

II
- a zoos
- b radios
- c echoes
- d solos
- e kimonos
- f heroes
- g dominoes
- h discos
- i yo yos
- j cuckoos

Page 5
I Active verbs are: a, b, d, f, i
Passive verbs are: c, e, g, h, j

II Many answers are possible.

Page 6
I
- a play
- b nibble
- c swims
- d gobble
- e fly
- f grow
- g are
- h needs

II
- a chases
- b deliver
- c eats
- d is
- e eat
- f delivers
- g chase
- h are

Page 7
I
- a **It was hot**, so we had a cold drink.
- b **My birthday is in October**, just before Hallowe'en.
- c On Friday, **we are going on holiday**.
- d Because it was so dark, **we took a torch**.
- e **We flew to Greece**, on an aeroplane.
- f **Susie is my best friend**, although I haven't known her very long.
- g **The window got broken**, but it was an accident.
- h **The shop was shut**, so we couldn't buy any sweets.

II a **It was raining hard**, so I took an umbrella.

b **The bus was late**, so we had to walk.
c Because it was Saturday, **we could play football all day**.
d **Max has chickenpox**, so he has to stay at home.
e **I play the guitar**, although I'm not very good.
f **Mum lost her keys**, so we had to call a locksmith.
g **Dad drank all the tea**, so he had to buy some more.
h **The television broke down**, so I read my book.

Page 8
I
- a boring, boredom
- b lightning, delight
- c impress, depression
- d machinist, machinery
- e breakfast, breakable
- f operation, cooperate
- g relative, relation
- h building, rebuild

II Many answers are possible, but your child's answers may include:
- a activity   action
- b mistake   retake
- c electrocute   electrify
- d signal   signature
- e reclaim   proclaim
- f publication   publicity
- g recover   discover
- h children   childhood

Page 9
I
- a peaceful
- b decide
- c city
- d careful
- e circuits
- f fearful
- g decimals
- h hopeful

II
- a cinema
- b colourful
- c harmful
- d circus
- e mouthful
- f decision
- g graceful
- h circle

Page 10
I
- a autograph
- b circumference
- c bifocals
- d telephoto
- e transparent
- f bilingual
- g circumstance
- h transplant
- i autobiography
- j telegraph

II
- a telephone
- b bicycle
- c automatic
- d translate
- e bilingual
- f automobile
- g television
- h transfer

Page 11
I
- a hot
- b empty
- c angry
- d wild
- e brave
- f old
- g exhausted
- h broke

II Many answers are possible.

Page 12
I
- a not acceptable
- b feeling unwell
- c very similar
- d absolutely thrilled
- e a great person to have around
- f just like a parent
- g raining very hard
- h happens very rarely

II Many answers are possible.

Page 13
I
- a 'Do you want to come back to my house after school?' asked Jamie.
- b 'That would be great,' replied Sasha. 'I'll have to check with my mum though.'
- c 'OK. If she says yes we could play with my new computer game.'
- d 'I'll go and ask her now,' said Sasha. 'See you in a minute.'

II Exact wording may vary.
'Have you done your homework?' asked Dad.
'Not all of it,' replied John.
Dad said, 'You'll have to do the rest after tea.'
'But I'm supposed to be playing football with Stephen,' complained John.
'Well, Stephen will just have to wait while you finish your homework,' replied Dad.

Page 14
I
- a proudly
- b timidly
- c rudely
- d confidently
- e gloomily
- f crossly
- g sleepily
- h sulkily

II Many answers are possible.

Page 15
I Many answers are possible.

II Many answers are possible.

Page 16
I
- a serial
- b aloud
- c board
- d waste
- e him
- f beech
- g steel
- h tale
- i leek
- j weak

II We took our **fair** (**fare**) and went to **bye** (**buy**) a ticket for the boat trip. The **son** (**sun**) shone brightly as our boat docked at the (**quay**) **key**. A sailor with blonde (**hair**) **hare** through (**threw**) a long **peace** (**piece**) of rope to another sailor standing by us. He **tide** (**tied**) it in a huge **not** (**knot**) to secure the boat. When the **mane** (**main**) gangplank appeared the passengers began to (**board**) **bored** the boat. We couldn't **weight** (**wait**) to set off!